P9-BYV-083

WAY-COOL

SPANiSH
Phrase Book

PASSPORT BOOKS

About this book

Jane Wightwick
had the idea

Wina Gunn
wrote the pages

Leila Gaafar (aged 10)
drew the first pictures in
each chapter

Robert Bowers
(not aged 10) drew the
other pictures, and
designed the book

Ana Bremon
did the Spanish stuff

Important things that **must** be included

First published in the United States in 2001 by

Passport Books
A division of The McGraw-Hill Companies.
4255 West Touhy Avenue, Lincolnwood (Chicago),
Illinois 60712-1975 U.S.A.

Copyright© 2000 by g-and-w PUBLISHING

All rights reserved. No part of this book may be
reproduced, stored in a retrieval system, or transmitted
in any form or by any means, electronic, mechanical,
photocopying, recording, or otherwise, without the
prior written permission of the copyright holders.

Printed in Singapore

Library of Congress Catalog Card Number: 00-135722

International Standard Book Number: 0-658-01691-1

01 02 03 04 05   15 14 13 12 11 10 9 8 7 6 5 4 3 2

What's inside

Making friends

How to be cool with the group

Wanna play?

Our guide to joining in everything from hide-and-seek to the latest electronic game

Feeling hungry

Order your favorite foods or go local

Looking good

Make sure you keep up with all those essential fashions

Hanging out

At the pool, beach, or theme park—don't miss out on the action

Pocket money

Spend it here!

Grown-up talk

blah! blah! blah! blah!

If you really, really have to!

Extra stuff

All the handy things— numbers, months, dates, days of the week

MAKING FRIENDS

me
yo 👄 yo

my snake
mi serpiente
👄 mee serpee-entay

my friend
mi amigo
👄 mee ameego

my friend
mi amiga
👄 mee ameea

my dog
mi perro
👄 mee pair-ro

6

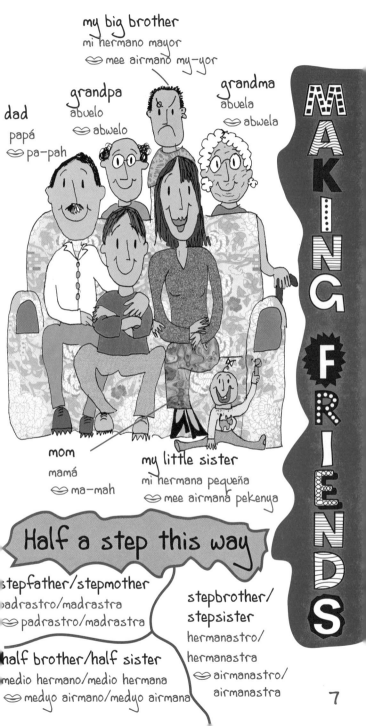

my big brother
mi hermano mayor
mee airmano my-yor

grandpa
abuelo
abwelo

grandma
abuela
abwela

dad
papá
pa-pah

mom
mamá
ma-mah

my little sister
mi hermana pequeña
mee airmana pekenya

Half a step this way

stepfather/stepmother
padrastro/madrastra
padrastro/madrastra

half brother/half sister
medio hermano/medio hermana
medyo airmano/medyo airmana

stepbrother/
stepsister
hermanastro/
hermanastra
airmanastro/
airmanastra

7

In Spanish you put an upside-down question mark before a question, as well as one right-side-up at the end. It's the same with exclamation marks.

¿Isn't that weird? ¡You bet!

How old are you?

¿Cuántos años tienes?

👄 kwantos anyos tee-enes

12 years old

Doce años

👄 dosay anyos

Happy birthday!

¡Cumpleaños feliz!

👄 koomplay-anyos faileess

What's your star sign?

¿Qué signo del zodiaco eres?

👄 kay signo del sodee-ako air-res

When's your birthday?

¿Cuándo es tu cumpleaños?

👄 kwando es too koomplay-anyos

Children sing "Happy Birthday" in Spanish to the same tune. Why don't you practice:

¡Cumpleaños Feliz!
¡Cumpleaños Feliz!

Star Signs

AQUARIUS
Jan. 21 – Feb. 19
Acuario 👄 akwaree-o

PISCES
Feb. 20 – Mar. 20
Piscis 👄 pees-sees

ARIES
Mar. 21 – Apr. 20
Aries 👄 a-rees

TAURUS
Apr. 21 – May 21
Tauro 👄 towro

GEMINI
May 22 – June 21
Geminis 👄 hemeenees

CANCER
June 22 – July 23
Cáncer 👄 kansair

LEO
July 24 – Aug. 23
Leo 👄 leo

VIRGO
Aug. 24 – Sep. 23
Virgo 👄 beergo

LIBRA
Sep. 24 – Oct. 23
Libra 👄 leebra

SCORPIO
Oct. 24 – Nov. 22
Escorpio 👄 eskorpee-o

SAGITTARIUS
Nov. 23 – Dec. 21
Sagitario 👄 sa-heetaree-o

CAPRICORN
Dec. 22 – Jan. 20
Capricornio 👄 kapreecomee-o

11

12

soccer
el fútbol
👄 el footbol

rollerskating/rollerblading
el patinaje en línea
👄 el patee-nahay en leenya

music
la música
👄 la mooseeka

electronic games
los juegos electrónicos
👄 los hway-gos elektroneekos

tv
la tele
👄 la taylay

comics
los tebeos
👄 los taybayos

teddy bears
los ositos de peluche
👄 los oseetos day peloochay

school
el colegio
👄 el kolay-heeyo

spiders
las arañas
👄 las aranyas

13

What's your ...?
¿Cuál es tu ... ?
👄 kwal es too ...

favorite group
grupo preferido
👄 groopo prefereedo

favorite color
color preferido
👄 kol-lor prefereedo

→ Page 51

favorite food
comida preferida
👄 komeeda prefereeda

favorite team
equipo preferido
👄 ekeepo prefereedo

animal

favorite animal
animal preferido
👄 anee-mal prefereedo

dog
el perro
👄 el pair-ro

cat
el gato
👄 el gato

snake
la serpiente
👄 la serpee-entay

guinea pig
la cobaya
👄 la kob-eye-a

hamster
el hámster
👄 el ahmstair

parakeet
el periquito
👄 el peree-keeto

My little doggy goes *guau guau!*

A doggy (that's "guauguau" in baby language) doesn't say "woof, woof" in Spanish; it says *"guau, guau"* (*gwa-oo, gwa-oo*). A Spanish bird says *"pío, pío"* (*pee-o, pee-o*) and "cock-a-doodle-do" in Spanish chicken-speak is *"kikirikí"* (*kee-kee ree-kee*). But a cat does say *"miaow"* and a cow *"moo"* whether they're speaking Spanish or English!

science
las ciencias
👄 las see-en-see-as

history
la historia
👄 la eestoreeya

School rules!

In Spanish-speaking countries, many children have to wear a uniform to school, and discipline is quite strict. On the other hand, they enjoy long vacation breaks: about 10 weeks in the summer and another 5–6 weeks during the school year. But before you turn green with envy, you might not like the mounds of "**tareas para las vacaciones**" (*taray-ahs para las bakasee-yones*); that's "vacation homework!" And if you fail your exams, the teachers could make you repeat the whole year with your little sister!

Gossip

Can you keep a secret?

¿Puedes guardar un secreto?

🗣 pwedes gwardar oon sekreto

Do you have a boyfriend (a girlfriend)?

¿Tienes novio (novia)?

🗣 tee-enes nobyo (nobya)

An OK guy/An OK girl

Un chavo bueno/Una chava buena 🗣 oon chabo bwayno/ oona chaba bwayna

Way bossy!

¡Qué mandón!

🗣 kay man-don (boy)

¡Qué mandona!

🗣 kay man-dona (girl)

He/She's nutty!

¡Está como una cabra!

🗣 esta komo oona kabra

That means "He/She's like a goat!"

"I'm not like that at all!"

What a creep!

¡Qué malasombra!

🗣 kay malas-sombra

You won't make many friends saying this!

Bug off!
¡Vete a la porra!
☞ betay a la porra

Shut up!
¡Cállate!
☞ kigh-yatay

If you're fed up with someone, and you want to say something like "you silly …!" or "you stupid …!", you can start with *"pedazo de"* (which actually means "piece of …") and add anything you like. What about …

Stupid banana!
¡Pedazo de plátano!
(pedaso day platano)

or …

Silly sausage!
¡Pedazo de salchicha!
(pedaso day salcheecha)

Take your pick. It should do the trick. You could also try *"¡Pedazo de idiota!"* (pedaso day eedee-ota). You don't need a translation here, do you?

You might have to say

Fudge!
¡Ostras!
os-stras

Rats!
¡Porras!
porras

"Did someone call us?"

las ostras

I'm fed up
¡Estoy harto! (boys)
¡Estoy harta! (girls)
estoy arto
estoy arta

That's enough!
¡Ya basta!
ya basta

I don't care
Me da igual
may da eegwal

Stop!
¡Para!
para

At last!
¡Por fin!
por feen

20

WANNA PLAY?

el elástico
👄 el elasteeko

el ping-pong
👄 el "ping-pong"

la pata coja
👄 la pata ko-ha

WANNA PLAY?

el Gameboy®
👄 el "gameboy"

las canicas
👄 las kaneekas

el yo-yo
👄 el "yo yo"

23

Do you want to play ...?
¿Quieres jugar ...?
👄 keyair-res hoogar

... foos-ball?
... al futbolín?
👄 al footboleen

... cards?
... a las cartas?
👄 a las kartas

... on the computer?
... con la computadora?
👄 kon la kompootadora

... tic-tac-toe?
... a las tres en raya?
👄 a las trays en righ-ya

... hide-and-seek?
... al escondite?
👄 al eskon-deetay

... catch?
... al balón?
👄 al ballon

24

Care for a game of **foal** or **donkey**?!

In Spain, you don't play "leap frog," you play "foal" —*el potro*. There is also a group version of this called "donkey"—*el burro*. This involves two teams. Team 1 lines up in a row with their heads down in the shape of a donkey. Team 2 takes turns to leap as far as they can onto the back of the "donkey." If the donkey falls over, Team 2 wins. If Team 2 touches the ground or can't leap far enough to get all the team on, then Team 1 wins—got that?! Spanish children will try to tell you this is enormous fun, but your parents might not be so happy about the bruises!

Make yourself heard

Electronic games

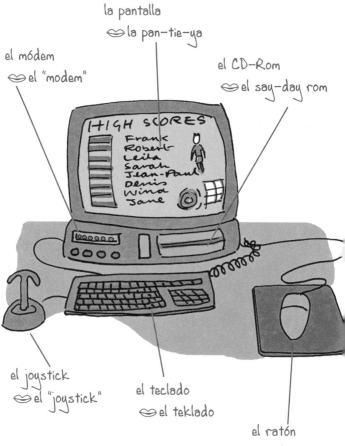

la pantalla
👄 la pan-tie-ya

el módem
👄 el "modem"

el CD-Rom
👄 el say-day rom

el joystick
👄 el "joystick"

el teclado
👄 el teklado

el ratón
👄 el rra-tone

28

What do I do?
¿Qué hay que hacer?
👄 kay eye kay asair

Show me
Enséñame
👄 ensay-nyamay

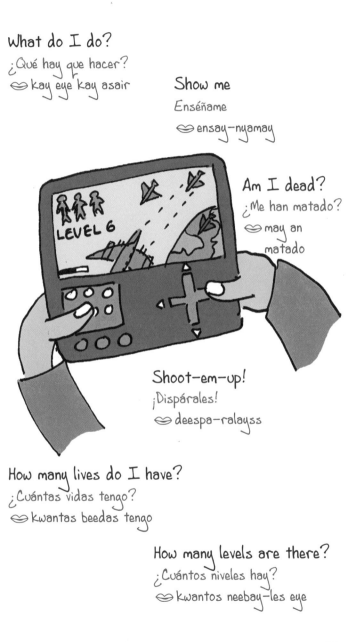

Am I dead?
¿Me han matado?
👄 may an matado

Shoot-em-up!
¡Dispárales!
👄 deespa-ralayss

How many lives do I have?
¿Cuántas vidas tengo?
👄 kwantas beedas tengo

How many levels are there?
¿Cuántos niveles hay?
👄 kwantos neebay-les eye

Non couch-potato activities!

tennis
el tenis
👄 el tenees

trampolining
el trampolín
👄 el trampoleen

bowling
los bolos
👄 los bol-los

swimming
la natación
👄 la nata-syon

hockey
el hockey
👄 el "hockey"

gymnastics
la gimnasia
👄 la heem-nasya

basketball el baloncesto
👄 el ballon-sesto

ballet
el ballet
👄 el ballay

and, of course, we haven't forgotten *"el fútbol!"*

31

soccer

shoes
las botas
👄 las botas

shin-pads
las espinilleras
👄 las espinee-yeras

ref
el árbitro
👄 el arbeetro

soccer gear
el equipo de fútbol
👄 el ekeepo day footbol

Good save!
¡Vaya parada!
👄 baya parada

crossbar
el larguero
👄 el largairo

goalpost
el palo
👄 el pallo

goal
el gol
👄 el gol

goalie
el portero
👄 el portairo

Pass!
¡Pasa!
👄 pasa

33

Keeping the others in line

Not like that!
¡Así no!
👄 asee no

You cheat!
¡Tramposo! (boys only)
¡Tramposa! (girls only)
👄 tramposo
   tramposa

I'm not playing anymore
Ya no juego
👄 ya no hwego

It's not fair!
¡No es justo!
👄 no es hoosto

Stop it!
¡No hagas eso!
👄 no agas eso

Impress your new friends with this!

You can show off to your new friends by practicing this tongue twister:

Tres tristes tigres comían trigo en un trigal

trays treestays teegrays comee-an treego en oon treegal

(This means "Three sad tigers ate wheat in a wheat field.")

Then see if they can do as well with this English one:

"She sells sea shells on the sea shore, but the shells she sells aren't sea shells, I'm sure."

For a rainy day

pack of cards
una baraja de cartas
☞ oona baraha
day kartas

my deal/your deal
yo doy/tú das
☞ yo doy/too das

king
el rey
☞ el rray

queen
la reina
☞ la rray-eena

jack
la jota
☞ la hota

joker
el komodín
☞ el komodee

tréboles
☞ trebol–les

corazones
☞ korason–nes

picas
☞ peekas

diamantes
☞ dee–amanta

Do you have the ace of swords?!

You might also see children playing with a different pack of cards. There are only 48 cards instead of 52, and the suits are also different. Instead of clubs, spades, diamonds, and hearts, there are gold coins (**oros**), swords (**espadas**), cups (**copas**), and batons (**bastos**).

chessboard
el tablero
👄 el tablairo

el alfil
👄 el alfeel

el caballo
👄 el kab-eye-o

el peón
👄 el pay-on

la torre
👄 la torray

el rey
👄 el rray

la reina
👄 la rray-eena

F
E
E
L
I
N
G
H
U
N
G
R
Y

hamburger
la hamburguesa
la amboorgaysa

fries
las papas fritas
las papas
freetas

ice cream
el helado
el elahdo

coke
una coca
oona koka

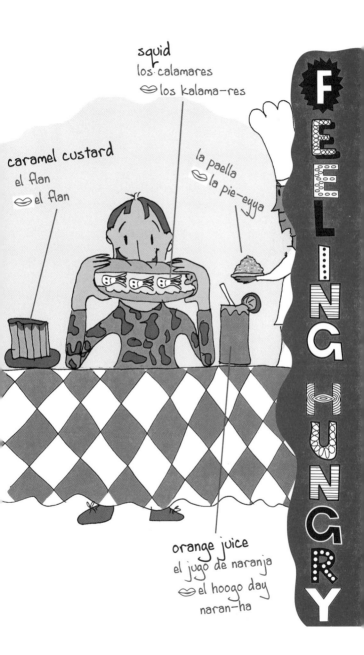

squid
los calamares
👄 los kalama-res

caramel custard
el flan
👄 el flan

la paella
👄 la pie-eyya

orange juice
el jugo de naranja
👄 el hoogo day
naran-ha

FEELING HUNGRY

39

Grub

I'm starving
Tengo un hambre de lobo
👄 tengo oon ambray day lobo

That means
"I have the
hunger of a wolf!"

Please can I have ...
Por favor, me da ...
👄 por fabor, may da

... a cream pastry
un bollo con nata
👄 oon boyo kon nata

... a croissant
un cruasán
👄 oon krwasan

... a sweet roll
una palmera
👄 oona palmayra

... a bread roll
un bollo
👄 oon boyo

... a waffle
un wafle
👄 oon wah–flay

los churros
👄 los choorros

These are wonderful sugary doughnut-like snacks. They are sold in cafés and kiosks and, in Spain, they come in a paper cone. They are also very popular for breakfast in winter, with thick hot chocolate (**chocolate con churros**).

You: Can I have some churros, Mom?

Mom: No. They'll make you fat and ruin your teeth.

You: But I think it's good to experience a foreign culture through authentic local food.

Mom: Oh, all right then.

Churros? *"¡Mm, mm!"* Garlic sandwich? *"¡Agh!"* If you're going to make food noises, you'll need to know how to do it properly in Spanish!

"Yum, yum!" is out in Spanish. You should say *"¡Mm, mm!"* And "Yuk!" is *"¡Agh!"* (pronounced "ag"), but be careful not to let adults hear you say this!

Drink up

I'm dying for a drink
Me muero de sed
🗣 may mwero day sed

... a coke
... una coca
🗣 oona koka

I'd like ...
Me apetece ...
🗣 may apay-taysay

... an orange juice
... un jugo de naranja
🗣 oon hoogo day naran-ha

... an apple juice
... un jugo de manzana
🗣 oon hoogo day mansana

In Mexico and other countries, the *limonadas* are carbonated. So instead of a plain lemonade, you're actually getting a lemon or lime soda-pop!

... **a lemonade**
una limonada
👄 oona leemonadah

... **water**
agua
👄 agwa

... **a milkshake**
... un batido de leche
👄 oon bateedo day laychay

You get your hot chocolate in a large cup (to dunk your churros in).

... **a hot chocolate**
... un chocolate
👄 oon chokolatay

Did you know?

A lot of children have hot chocolate for breakfast in the morning and some of them will dip their churros or bread in it. They get very soggy and Mom is sure not to like this!

44

Adventures in Eating!

If you're traveling in Mexico and Central America and you don't like hot, spicy food, a good question to know is **Es picante?** (*es peekantay*—"Is it spicy?"). If the answer is no, your tongue won't catch on fire!

And if you're hungry for comfort food, you can always ask for one of the following dishes:

noodle soup

sopa de fideos

☞ sopa day feeday-os

spaghetti

espaguetis

☞ espaghetees

… with meatballs

… con albóndigas

☞ kon albon-deegas

you can even ask for …

pizza

pizza

☞ peessa

nail polish
el esmalte para las uñas
el esmahltay para las oonyas

headband
la diadema
la dee-adema

braid
la trencita
la tren-seeta

bracelets
las pulseras
las poolsairas

crop top
la camiseta
la kameesa

belt
el cinturón
el seen-tooron

miniskirt
la minifalda
la minee-fald

shoes
los zapatos
los sapatos

bike
la bici
la beesee

LOOKING GOOD

46

cap
la gorra
🍃 la gorra

T-shirt
la camiseta
🍃 la kameeseta

tattoo
la calcomanía
🍃 la kalko-maneeya

jeans
los vaqueros
o
🍃 los bakayros

el walkman
🍃 el "walkman"

skateboard
el monopatín
🍃 el mono-pateen

tennis shoes
los deportivos
🍃 los daypor-teebos

LOOKING GOOD

47

That T-shirt please
Esa camiseta, por favor
🗣 esa kameeseta, por fabor

Cool tattoo!
¡Qué calcomanía más padre!
🗣 kay kalko-maneeya mass padray

The pink frilly one
La rosa con volantitos
🗣 la rosa kon bolanteetos

A braid, please
Una trencita, por favor
🗣 oona trenseeta, por fabor

The purple striped one
La morada de raya
🗣 la morada day righ-yas

Awesome miniskirt!
¡Vaya minifalda más chula!
🗣 baya meenee-falda mass choola

Where's my skateboard?
¿Dónde está mi monopatín?
🗣 donday esta mee mono-pateen

A pair of cowboys?

The word for jeans in Spanish (**los vaqueros** – *los bakayros*) actually means "cowboys" because they were the first people to wear these trousers.

48

spotted
de lunares
👄 day loona-res

flowery
de flores
👄 day flo-res

frilly
con volantitos
👄 kon bolanteetos

glittery
con brillos
👄 kon breeyos

striped
de rayas
👄 day righ-yas

49

jeans
los vaqueros
～los
bakayros

T-shirt
la camiseta
～la kameeset

sweatshirt
la sudadera
～la sooda-
dayra

tennis shoes
los deportivos
～los daypor-
teebos

dress
el vestido
～el bay-
steedo

pants
los pantalone
～los panta
lone-nes

skirt
la falda
～la falda

soccer shirt
la camiseta de fútbol
～la kameeseta
day footbol

shorts
los pantalones cortos
～los panta-lone-nes kortos

shoes
los zapatos
～los sapatos

50

Color this page yourself
(you can't expect us to do everything!)

colors
los colores
👄 los kolo-res

white
blanco
👄 blanko

green
verde
👄 berday

orange
naranja
👄 naranha

blue
azul
👄 asool

pink
rosa
👄 rossa

yellow
amarillo
👄 amareeyo

red
rojo
👄 roho

purple
morado
👄 morado

black
negro
👄 naygro

51

What should we do?

¿Qué hacemos?

👄 kay asay-mos

Can I come?

¿Puedo ir?

👄 pwedo eer

Where do you all hang out?

¿Por dónde salen ustedes?

👄 por donday salen oos-tedays

That's mega!

¡Qué emoción!

👄 kay aymosee-yon

I'm (not) allowed

(No) me dejan

👄 (no) may day-han

Let's go back
Regresemos
👄 regray-saymos

That gives me goose bumps (or "chicken flesh" in Spanish!)
Eso me pone la carne de gallina
👄 eso may ponay la karnay day gayeena

I'm scared
Tengo miedo
👄 tengo mee-aydo

I'm bored to death
Me muero de aburrimiento
👄 may mwero day aburree-mee-ento

That's funny
Te ríes cantidad
👄 tay reeyes kanteedad

HOUSE OF MIRRORS

55

sea
el mar
👄 el mar

beach
la playa
👄 la playa

and castle
castillo de arena
👄 el casteeyo day arayna

towel
la toalla
👄 la toe-aya

bathing suit
el bañador
👄 el banyador

bucket
el cubo
👄 el koobo

snorkel
el tubo
👄 el toobo

shovel
la pala
👄 la palla

shells
las conchas
👄 las konechas

It's going swimmingly!

How to make a splash in Spanish!

PLOF

Let's hit the swimming pool
¿Vamos a la piscina?
👄 bamos a la peeseena

Can you swim (underwater)?
¿Sabes nadar (debajo del agua)?
👄 sabays nadar (debaho del agwa)

Me too/I can't
Yo también/Yo no
👄 yo tambeeyen/yo no

Can you dive?
¿Te sabes tirar de cabeza?
👄 tay sabays teerar day kabaysa

I'm getting changed
Me estoy cambiando
👄 may estoy kambee-ando

... backstroke
de espalda
👄 day espalda

Can you swim ...?
¿Sabes nadar ...?
👄 sabays nadar

... butterfly
a mariposa
👄 a mareeposa

... crawl
a crol
👄 a krohl

... breaststroke
a braza de pecho
👄 a brasa day paycho

slide
el tobogán
👄 el tobogan

goggles
las gafas
👄 las gafas

59

Downtown

Do you know the way?
¿Sabes el camino?
👄 sabays el kameeno

Is it far?
¿Está lejos? 👄 esta lay-hos

Are we allowed in here?
¿Nos dejan entrar aquí?
👄 nos day-han entrar akee

Let's ask
Vamos a preguntar
👄 bamos a pray-goontar

Pooper-scoopers on wheels!

In Spain you might see bright green-and-white motorcycles with funny vacuum cleaners on the side riding around town scooping up the dog poop. The people riding the bikes look like astronauts! (Well, you'd want protection too, wouldn't you?)

playground
el patio de recreo
👄 el pateeyo day rekrayo

slide
el tobogán
👄 el tobogan

park
el parque
👄 el parkay

swings
los columpios
👄 los koloom-peeyos

bus
el autobús
👄 el owtoboos

car
el coche
👄 el kochay

You can show off your "street smarts" to your new friends by using some slang.
A junky old car is *"una cafetera"* (*oona cafaytayra*), which means "coffee pot!" Try this: *"¡Vaya cafetera!"* (*baya cafaytayra*—"What an old clunker!").

61

Picnics

I hate wasps
Odio las avispas
☞ odeeyo las abeespas

Move over!
¡Apártate!
☞ apar–tatay

bread
el pan
☞ el pan

Let's sit here
¿Nos sentamos aquí?
☞ nos sentamos ak

napkin
la servilleta
☞ la serbeeyeta

ham
el jamón
☞ el hamon

cheese
el queso
☞ el kayso

yogurt
el yogur
☞ el yogur

chips
las papas fritas
☞ las papas freetas

drinks
las bebidas
👄 las bebeedas

knife
el cuchillo
👄 el koocheeyo

spoon
la cuchara
👄 la koochara

fork
el tenedor
👄 el tenaydor

wasps
las avispas
👄 las abeespas

bees
las abejas
👄 las abayhas

bzzzz

ants
las hormigas
👄 las ormeegas

All the fun of the fair

slide
el tobogán
🗣 el tobogan

Ferris wheel
la noria
🗣 la noreeya

house of mirrors
la casa de los espejos
🗣 la kasa day los espayhos

bumper cars
los coches de choque
🗣 los kochays day chokay

Let's go on this
¿Nos montamos en éste?
🗣 nos montamos en estay

Spend it here

candy
los caramelos
👄 los karamaylos

T-shirts
las camisetas
👄 las kameeseta

P O C K E T M O N E Y

toys
los juguetes
👄 los hoogaytays

el tendero
👄 el tendayr

books
los libros
≋ los leebros

mobile
el móvil
≋ el mobeel

pencils
los lápices
≋ los lapeeses

POCKET MONEY

What does that sign say?

Carnicería

carnicería
butcher shop
👄 karneesereeya

pastelería
cake shop
👄 pastele-
reeya

Pastelería

panadería
bakery
👄 panadereeya

Panadería

confitería
candy store
👄 confeete-
reeya

Verdulería

papelería
office supplies
👄 papelereeya

PAPELERIA

verdulería
grocery store
👄 berdoole-
reeya

Money talk

Money has different names and values, depending on the country you visit.

boutique
clothes store
👄 booteek

Boutique

Spain = **pesetas** (*paysaytas*)
Mexico = **pesos** (*paysos*)
Guatemala = **quetzales** (*ketsalays*)
Costa Rica = **colones** (*kolonays*)

Of course, you must exchange your **dollares** (*doe-larays*) at a bank (**banco**—*banko*) or currency exchange (**casa de cambio**—*kasa day kam-beeyo*). But if you're in Puerto Rico, you're all set—the money is the same!

68

69

Sweet heaven!

I love this shop
Me encanta esta tienda
👄 may enkanta esta tee-enda

Let's get some candy
Vamos a comprar dulces
👄 bamos a comprar doolsays

Let's get some ice cream
Vamos por un helado
👄 bamos por oon aylado

lollipops
las piruletas
👄 las peerooletas

a bar of chocolate
una tableta de chocolate
👄 oona tableta day chokolatay

chewing gum
el chicle
👄 el cheeklay

If you really want to look cool, but end up with lots of fillings, ask for:

regaliz
(regaleess)

soft licorice sticks, available in red or black

nubes (noobes)

soft marshmallow candies in different shades (**nubes** means "clouds")

jamones
(hamon—nes)

fruity, fizzy gum in the shape of hams ("ham" is **jamón**)

Chupa—chups® (choopa—choops)

lollipops famous all over the world, but they come from Spain

polvos pica-pica (polvos peeka peeka)

tangy fizzy sherbet sold in small packets with a lollipop to dip in

kilométrico (keelomay—treeko)

chewing gum in a strip like dental floss—pretend to the adults that you're flossing your teeth!

71

Other things you could buy
(that won't ruin your teeth!)

What are you getting?
¿Qué te vas a comprar?
👄 kay tay bas a komprar

That toy, please
Ese juguete, por favor
👄 esay hoogaytay, por fabor

Two postcards, please
Dos postales, por favor
👄 dos postal-
les, por fabor

How much is that?
¿Cuánto cuesta?
👄 kwanto kwesta

This is garbage
Esto es una porquería
👄 esto es oona
porkayreeya

This rules
¡Chévere!
👄 chay-bairay

72

... colored pencils
... lápices de colores
☞ lapeesays day kolo-rès

I'm getting ...
Voy a comprar ☞ boy a comprar

... stamps
... sellos
☞ seyos

... felt-tip pens
... rotuladores
☞ rotoolado-res

Rotuladores

... a pen
... un boli
☞ oon bolee

... a cassette
... una cinta
☞ oona seenta

... a CD
... un compacto
☞ oon compacto

... comics
... tebeos
☞ taybayos

For many years Spain's favorite comics have been *Mortadelo y Filemón*, two accident-prone TIA agents (<u>not</u> CIA) and *Zipi y Zape*, two very naughty twins. Children also like to read *Mafalda*, an Argentinian comic, *Carlitos y Snoopy* (Charlie Brown & Snoopy), *Tintin*, *Astérix*, and *¿Dónde está Wally?* (Where's Waldo?).

75

Help!

Something has dropped/broken
Algo se ha caído/roto
☞ algo say a kigh-eedo/roto

Please
Por favor
☞ por fabor

Can you help me?
¿Me puedes ayudar?
☞ may pwedes ayoodar

Where's the mailbox?
¿Dónde está el buzón?
☞ donday esta el booson

Where are the toilets?
¿Dónde están los aseos?
☞ donday estan los asayos

I can't manage it
No puedo
👄 no pwedo

Could you pass me that?
¿Me pasas eso?
👄 may pasas eso

What time is it?
¿Qué hora es?
👄 kay ora es

Come and see
Ven a ver
👄 ben a bair

May I look at your watch?
¿Me deja que mire su reloj?
👄 may deha kay meeray soo reloh

77

Lost for words

... my ticket
mi billete
👄 mee beeyaytay

I've lost ...
He perdido ...
👄 eh perdeedo

... my bike
mi bici
👄 mee beesee

... my parents
mis padres
👄 mees padrays

... **my shoes**
mis zapatos
👄 mees sapatos

... **my money**
mi dinero
👄 mee deenayro

... **my sweater**
mi suéter
👄 mee swetair

... **my watch**
mi reloj
👄 mee reloh

... **my jacket**
mi chaqueta
👄 mee chakayta

79

ADULTS ONLY!

Show this page to adults who can't seem to make themselves clear (it happens). They will point to a phrase, you read what they mean, and you should all understand each other perfectly.

No te preocupes
Don't worry

Siéntate aquí
Sit down here

¿Tu nombre y apellidos?
What's your name and surname?

¿Cuántos años tienes?
How old are you?

¿De dónde eres?
Where are you from?

¿Dónde te alojas?
Where are you staying?

¿Dónde te duele?
Where does it hurt?

¿Eres alérgico a algo?
Are you allergic to anything?

Está prohibido
It's forbidden

Tiene que acompañarte un adulto
You have to have an adult with you

Voy por alguien que hable inglés
I'll get someone who speaks English

Knock, knock.

Who's there?

Uno.

Uno who?

Unos where I got this crummy joke!

uno 👄 oono

dos 👄 dos

tres 👄 trays

cuatro 👄 kwatro

cinco 👄 seenko

seis 👄 sayis

siete 👄 see-etay

ocho 👄 ocho

nueve 👄 nwebay

diez 👄 deeyess

once 👄 onsay

doce 👄 dosay

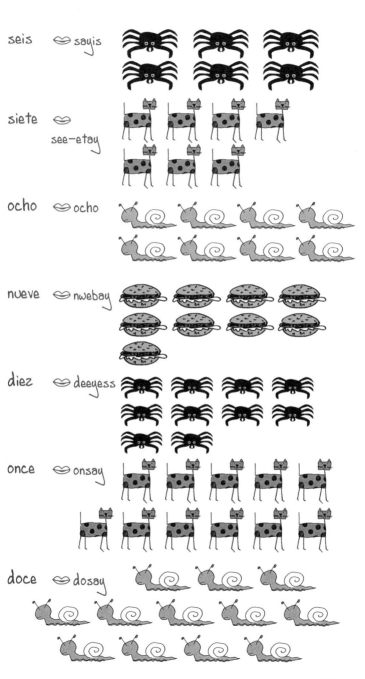

83

13	trece	*tresay*
14	catorce	*katorsay*
15	quince	*keensay*
16	dieciséis	*deeyesee sayis*
17	diecisiete	*deeyesee see-etay*
18	dieciocho	*deeyesee ocho*
19	diecinueve	*deeyesee nwebay*
20	veinte	*baintay*

I f you want to say "twenty-two," "sixty-five," and so on, you can just put the two numbers together like you do in English. But don't forget to add the word for "and" (**y**, pronounced *ee*) in the middle:

32	**treinta y dos**	*traynta ee dos*
54	**cincuenta y cuatro**	*seenkwenta ee kwatro*
81	**ochenta y uno**	*ochenta ee oono*

30	treinta	*traynta*
40	cuarenta	*kwarenta*
50	cincuenta	*seenkwenta*
60	sesenta	*saysenta*
70	setenta	*saytenta*
80	ochenta	*ochenta*
90	noventa	*nobenta*
100	cien	*seeyen*

1st	primero	*preemairo*
2nd	segundo	*segoondo*
3rd	tercero	*tersayro*
4th	cuarto	*kwarto*
5th	quinto	*keento*
6th	sexto	*sexto*
7th	séptimo	*septeemo*
8th	octavo	*octabo*
9th	noveno	*nobayno*
10th	décimo	*dayseemo*

Want a date?

If you want to say a date in Spanish, you don't need to use 1st, 2nd, etc. Just say

Lunes	Martes	Miércoles	Jueves	Viernes	Sábado	Domingo
		1	2	3	4	5
6	7	8	9	10	11	12
13	14	15	16	17	18	19
20	21	22	23	24	25	26
27	28	29	30			

the ordinary number followed by *de* (*day*):

| uno de marzo | (1st of March) |
| diez de Julio | (10th of July) |

March	marzo	*marso*
April	abril	*abreel*
May	mayo	*my-yo*

June	junio	*hooneeyo*
July	julio	*hooleeyo*
August	agosto	*agosto*

September	septiembre	*septee-embray*
October	octubre	*octoobray*
November	noviembre	*nobee-embray*

December	diciembre	*deesee-embray*
January	enero	*enayro*
February	febrero	*febrayro*

primavera   *preemabayra*

verano   *berano*

otoño   *otonyo*

invierno   *eenbee-erno*

Monday	lunes	*loon-nes*
Tuesday	martes	*mar-tes*
Wednesday	miércoles	*mee-erkol-les*
Thursday	jueves	*hoo-ebes*
Friday	viernes	*bee-er-nes*
Saturday	sábado	*sabado*
Sunday	domingo	*domeengo*

By the way, many kids have a two-and-a-half hour lunch break! Time enough for lunch and a siesta. But school doesn't finish until 5 o'clock!

Good times

It's ...
Son ...
🗨 sonn

(five) o'clock
las (cinco)
🗨 las (seenko)

quarter after (two)
las (dos) y cuarto
🗨 las (dos) ee kwarto

quarter to (four)
las (cuatro) menos cuarto
🗨 las (kwatro) menos kwarto

half past (three)
las (tres) y media
🗨 las (trays) ee medya

five after (ten)
las (diez) y cinco
👄 las (deeyes) ee seenko

twenty after (eleven)
las (once) y veinte
👄 las onsay ee baintay

ten to (four)
las (cuatro) menos diez
👄 las (kwatro) menos
deeyes

twenty to (six)
las (seis) menos veinte
👄 las sayis menos baintay

Watch out for "one o'clock." It's different from the other times. If you want to say "It's one o'clock," you have to say **Es la una** (*es la oona*). "It's half past one" is **Es la una ee medya** (*es la oona ee medya*), and so on.

91

morning
mañana
👄 la manyana

midday
mediodía
👄 el medyo-deeya

afternoon
la tarde
👄 la tarday

midnight
la medianoche
👄 la medya-
nochay

evening
la noche
👄 la nochay

92

now
ahora
👄 a-ora

night
la noche
👄 la nochay

today
hoy
👄 oy

3 4 5 6
10 11 12 13

yesterday
ayer
👄 ayair

tomorrow
mañana
👄 manyana

Weather wise

Can we go out?
¿Podemos salir fuera?
👄 podaymos saleer fwera

It's hot
Hace calor
👄 asay kalor

It's cold
Hace frío
👄 asay freeyo

It's a horrible day
Hace un día horrible
👄 asay oon deeya orreeblay

It's raining seas!

In Spanish it doesn't rain "cats and dogs,"
it rains "seas!" That's what they say when
it's raining
really heavily:

¡Está lloviendo
a mares! *esta
yobeeyendo
a ma-res*

It's windy
Hace viento
👄 asay beeyento

It's sunny
Hace sol
👄 asay sol

It's raining
Está lloviendo
👄 esta yobeeyendo

It's snowing
Está nevando
👄 esta nebando

I'm soaked
Estoy empapado (boy)/
Estoy empapada (girl)
👄 estoy empapado/empapada

It's nice
Hace buen tiempo
👄 asay bwen teeyempo

95